dystopia unplugged

please talk back

blake more

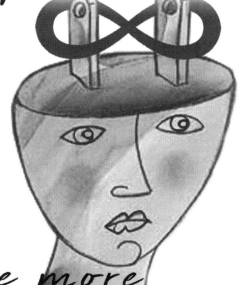

© 2024 blake more
All rights reserved

ISBN: 979-8-9903248-0-0
More You Press

words, layout & design by blake more

No part of this work may be reproduced or transmitted in any form or by any means, electronic or mechanical, including photocopying and recording, or by any information storage or retrieval system without the prior written permission of the copyright owner.

b more creations
post office box 765
point arena, ca 95468
bmoreyou.net
snakelyone.com

dystopia unplugged

please talk back

blake more

Contents

Introduction.........7
Convene Supervene.........13
Dispatch From the Ledge.........15
Reaching Deep.........18
Pass the Pandemic, a Teachers Saga.........20
Another Day Alone.........22
Beautiful Shit Show.........23
Dropper Full of Wake Up.........26
Fly Om.........29
Big Daddy Patriarchy.........30
A Message to the Future.........33
Science of Deep.........34
Do Butterflies Hug.........35
Anti-Ode to a Mask.........37
Pin Striping the Firmament.........38
Bespoke Suburbia.........40
A Lot of Hate to Love.........42
He-ART-I-Facts.........46
The Big Lie.........48
Anti-Ode to Mr. Global.........52
Ho Ho Hum.........54
In the New Year.........56
www.TV.........57
Unzip the Mind Bag.........61
First Amendment in the Time of Canceling.........63
Dear Prussian Prudence.........67
Willful Ignorance.........69
Do You Believe.........70
Drink a Little Poison or Go Thirsty.........72
Start Making Sense.........74
Ode to Emotional Intelligence.........75
Tea and Tango, for Point Arena.........76
Love Is My Currency.........78
Peace Be Kind.........80
Forgiveness 101.........83
Seeing Abundance.........85
Wake the Bear.........86
Tolerance Is Bliss.........88
You Are You.........90
Please Talk Back.........92

Introduction

Well, here they are. My past three plus years of poems – my brain during the "pandemic" that took over life in ways never imagined possible. These are the words that sent friends running, some toward me, others away from me. As I write this to you today, all but a very few of my friends and employers have forgiven my stand and allowed me back into their circles. I am grateful for that, because it means they are willing to acknowledge a choice that was nearly legislated out of possibility.

Holding a line is not easy, but I am proud of my sovereignty, as it shows that I value my inner knowing more than group approval. Well, I guess I've known that for a while, but it feels good to witness myself in practice. Like always, poetry is my spirit animal.

The poetry in this book helped me withstand the finger-pointing, the dinner parties I couldn't attend, the clubs and festivals that wouldn't admit me, the unexpected political & cultural exile, town talk about my selfishness and the barrage of *anti-science-flat-earther* accusations planted like a seed between the ears of loved ones by none other than our national health secretary.

These poems gave me an outlet for an expression I was not supposed to make in polite company. Art provides wiggle room, and I took every elbow space I could to push back at the intolerance I faced every day. I read these poems aloud to anyone who would listen – on the phone, in grocery store parking lots, around campfires, on my radio shows and at our monthly poetry & jazz event. It was scary, and even so, I stayed true to my heart and did my very best to forgive others for what they chose to do and say, even when it alarmed the frick out of me.

I cried, winced and laughed out loud as I wrote these poems. I'm presenting them in chronological order because they provide a map of my descent into the incredulity of it all. I also include web links at the end of all the poems that I turned into "video poems". You can check out all of my video poems at **https://www.bmoreyou.net/category/video**

A couple of poems, like "The Big Lie" and "www.TV" were written in a funneled frenzy at 3am and needed almost no editing. Others, like "Big Daddy Patriarchy" and "Beautiful Shit Show", came with a witty impish elfin voice who poked and cajoled me into metabolizing some of the feelings that had nowhere to go.

Some poems were written in classrooms or on Zoom while the students were doing their own writing to the prompts I gave them; "Anti-Ode to a Mask" and "Anti-Ode to Mr. Global" were both written during my very first in-person high school class since early 2020, shortly after the mask mandates were lifted for public schools. The lesson was anti-odes, and as students were writing, I realized that in a room of 26 people, only me and two others were showing our mouths – again, poetry offered a reasonable pressure release valve.

A few poems were written for civic or organizational events, like the poem "Peace be Kind" that I was asked to write for the Point Arena Independence Day parade, the first one in two years. My only requirement from the mayor was to "be nice". I think I did a good job.

> here we are/ still alive/ opening ourselves to the world/ we nearly let go/ hugging each other/ inviting friends back to our tables/ this tender community/ realizing the only way out/ is through/ looking into the horror/ recognizing its beauty

In hindsight, I believe the dark days most of us lived through were necessary. True change does not happen without a catalyst, and while the usual players are still trying to manipulate us back into the Truman Show, many have become unwilling to revert back to the blissful ignorance of 2019.

We were collectively red pilled, and while that *Matrix* analogy is grossly over-used, it has become cliché for a reason – it expresses how we feel. Fortunately, I was red-pilled before there was a red-pill, so I am not surprised that two weeks to flatten the curve is still lingering today.

There is no stopping the inevitable cycle of transformation, and never before have I been so comfortable with the free fall of it all. Unsure if our outcome will be halcyon or shatter, our planet spins new shadows, as old ones rise to tell their stories, rushing, falling, thrusting. I am a utopist, so even my most brutal poetry shines light on what is possible when we choose love.

The last few years have stretched the boundaries of my commitment to optimism and sanguinity, to hope and my belief in the social, cultural, emotional intelligence of humanity. The life I once held dear shifted so drastically inside I had no choice but to forge something new outside. This new is less comfortable but feels more authentic and requires the kind of deep diving that forever alters a person. This truly hard work has brought out an essence in me that I thought only music could evoke.

Genuine leadership must come from within, and for me, I'm committed to embodying this awareness so I can stand tall as a beacon of freedom and love.

I pray that you are feeling empowered and are doing what it takes to keep your heart open and your head clear. My hope is that as you read these words, you allow yourself to contemplate our society, our culture, its leaders with inquisitive eyes, realizing that so much of what we have been told begs a second meditation.

Everything we need to transform our world is within us, and the more we can turn off the distracting, petty-pretty-sexy-entertaining screens of control, the sooner we can reclaim our creative value and shift the narrative to one of unity and peace.

Our innate nature is being used to distract and control us. Few of us actually think *humans are stupid and need more authoritarian control.* More of us believe that humans are innately good. This understanding begets a willingness to do whatever it takes to keep us *all safe*. That is how our freedoms and personal choices got taken away: Our compassion was literally weaponized against us.

Afraid of loosing the people we love most, we dutifully followed a bramble path, defining our virtue via divisiveness, trusting the institutions we used to doubt, ignoring the rubble of relationships at our feet, telling ourselves how good and blameless we've been because we are righteous and doing what we are supposed to do. What is best for our nation and its citizens. What smart, caring, kind people do. What people who trust science do.

You may think everything on these pages so far is abject rubbish, and that is your right. But thankfully, in early 2024, I am still allowed to write and publish my treasured compost. Yet inquisitive, skeptical people like me are increasingly censored, shadow banned, demonetized and deplatformed for words that go against the accepted "consensus narrative." This is the dystopia we are facing.

I want to hear from you. What works, what does not, what makes you think, what shuts you down. Yell at me, cry with me, laugh at me. Just don't mute me or yourself. Silence is a death sentence. Words are a lifeline. I hope this book opens your throat and draws out insights you can offer others. It is time to reach across the prescribed divisions and find each other again.

Understand, that I am a funnel, as all poets are, and I trust my inner voice enough to offer it to you. I ask that you please read with love and use your heart ears to look for our common ground. Tolerance is the way forward, and I hope you join me in the movement to unplug the dystopia closing in on us! Now is the time to talk back!

Blake More, March 2024

Convene Supervene

I awoke this morning thinking about all the people I love
and how I want to call each one of you
and say, it is okay, we'll be okay, we are okay
we are light
we are love
we are collective consciousness
pushing itself from a deep dream of frenzied sleep
amid corona messages from corporations
with generic templates
news briefs about bipartisan senators selling stock
as they reassure the public
we will all be just fine
come May, or maybe by October
posts of top CEOs jumping out of the game
in the nick of time
their golden parachutes pirouetting in the wind
of this worldwide panic pandemic
as if they are immune

maybe they are, in their bunkers in South Dakota or Panama
or whatever middle earth conspiracy story
appeals to your creative imagination
counting their one percent while the rest of us duke it out
over toilet paper and frozen pizza
holy water replaced by hand sanitizer

lives constructed carefully or carelessly
on the brink of virtual collapse
safety nets revealing their rabbit holes
bystanders wondering who among us will slip through
as we plummet into an unknown
embraced by those who've been training
to meet this moment for decades

this is no time to fear
because something here is real
real as the air we share

Unplugged ~ 13

the surfaces without touch
the missing hugs
as real as dolphins returning
balconies breaking out
in cohesive song

as real as this blue earth
making up point zero-zero-zero-three percent
of the total mass of a solar system
sharing the milky way with 40 billion
potentially habitable planets like our own

as real as these bodies
unfurling like springtime ferns
in the dawn of our awakening

social distancing without euphemism
is social isolation
i.e., mediation
nothing else to do
but make love inside ourselves
with lungs and isotopes
with inhale exhale
feeding the antibodies
with able-bodied thoughts
tell them *we got this*
and we will
tell them *we got this*
and we do

view blake's "Convene Supervene" poem movie here: *https://www.bmoreyou.net/convene-supervene-a-covid-19-poem*

Dispatch from the Ledge

We put our masks on
prepared to dance back out
into the murky future ball
six feet from each other
fist bumping, keeping our spit to ourselves
spending our tiny pennies in the few shops
allowed to gingerly proffer wares
over the threshold of change
we spend hours
gritting teeth over
in Odyssean attempts
to let the government help us
help ourselves

we celebrate, gently at first
at the idea of being allowed to gather
perhaps dine in a half empty restaurant
toast a friendship in person
visit a grandchild

we are told life is forever changed
that we will have to stay away from each other
give up hugs for at least a year
smile behind cloth
comprehending an inkling of the burka
to save lives, *yes to save lives* they tell us
which we all so very much want to do
sequestering ourselves in homes
as long as we have them
others braving necessary cash registers
to kick start this lopsided economy

hold on we do
taking heart in regenerating ozone layers
goats herding over highways
gorging on information
until our brains crack

wild weeds wending
their way into novel perspectives
scientists, researchers, health warriors
on the frontlines of this crisis
offering information counter to official news angles
madly forwarding emails
in hopes they'll be captured
before disappearing from the public record
to protect the sanctity of our minds
as if citizens cannot tell the difference
between what is real
what is not

maybe they can't
but this fact cannot be disputed
our mighty dispensers of free screen entertainment
have acknowledged their collusion with red boxes
slanted smiles admonishing
those who violate guidelines
but WHO decides fake news?

people say we'll never be China
that Hitler did not exist
that the pharmaceutical companies
did not cause the opioid crisis

now I understand
how easy it is to tether oneself to belief
forsake all else

human's have been doing it for millennia
clubbing each other, dropping bombs,
broadcasting messages, liking posts
to make us feel better about our superior opinions
while the villainous other side does the same thing
the duality river becoming an ocean
with quarantined cruise ships
on their respective banks
politicians diving between them
for billionaire scraps

16 ~ *Dystopia*

like gulls swarming a seine net

but ask a Washington insider
with no allegiance to a false flag
she will tell you the sanctimonious masquerade
is made of smoke
as this B-grade, dystopian sci-fi movie
rolls the mirror toward its final credits

the real masks are coming off
revealing red and blue guises
similar to those of history

do not be alarmed
the lines taped on the sidewalks
cannot stop us from talking
our innocence was lost long ago
perhaps we are ready to acknowledge it

an expanse is forming
one with no walls
no polarities
a birds' eye vista witnessing
corruption and fortitude
with equal eyes

we are all first
in this translucent crystal
of now

view the "Dispatch from the Ledge" poem movie here:
https://www.bmoreyou.net/dispatch-from-the-ledge-life-in-the-time-of-covid

Reaching Deep
~ for the youth stuck at home

I halfway remember the first time
my grandmother states
only boring people get bored
I recall thinking—
clueless, dumb—didn't she see
I am an LA kid stuck
in the farmlands of Arkansas
for an entire summer
the mighty Pacific
replaced by a garden hose
row after row of corn
nobody interesting to play with
the nearest mall 90 minutes by station wagon?

days wear on,
tedious, annoying, endless
around month one I grow *bored with myself*
rise from my sleeping, moping, complaining couch
go outside

To my surprise I notice bright green pods
dangling from a wooden fence
small round berries redder than any Macy's sweater
the air smells of fresh dirt
claps of thunder offer torrents of warm rain
that feel as good as any ocean

For the rest of the visit, I swim with the sky
dance to the sound of cicadas in the evening
I eat peaches off the branch, lettuce from the ground
I sit under the massive shade of a pecan tree
draw the creatures of my dreams
I write postcards to friends, letters to my parents
I go to bed tired, wake up hungry to go outside again
my grandparents notice

my suppertime smiles
but remain silent
perhaps they understand what I do not
that nature's DNA
is rooting the marrow of my skin
forever altering my churlish quest
for perpetual entertainment
immediate glitter and rush
of movies, sleep overs,
candy bars from the corner store
replaced by magical plant brews
and the simple,
slow
syrup
of time

Unplugged ~ 19

Pass the Pandemic
~ a Teachers Saga

Feel it, I say
the words crashing through like an airplane
looking to land on the tarmac of time
imaginary ears nodding
drinking in fearlessness
after wandering through deserts of whitewater
why me's lining the sky
like contrails of ancestral poison
these are the days of heart hoofs
and other palpitations demanding the fullness of sound
I say to cartoon characters, fish, cats, skulls and anime
representing what we used to call students
sitting in desks and chairs

the classroom teacher and I appear to be hosting a podcast
unsure if we have an audience
but praying someone is out there
we speak of the enlightenment
the advent of the printing press
how true change
historically comes from the bottom up

a student is asked to read John Gay's "Green Sleeves"
we ask for comments, a note in the chat
nothing
another reads
"On Being Brought from Africa to America" by Phyllis Wheatley,
crickets
I play Maya Angelou's "And Still I Rise",
Gill Scott Heron's "the Revolution Will not be Televised"
pins dropping

I remind
books are weapons for good and ill
that these days discernment is the challenge

quiet as church mice
they, like so many, appear unaware
that the people's history is being written
alongside the Foxes and NBC BS
of the sell out alphabet outlets
perpetuating the corporatized version of reality
while thousands of busy researcher elves
from all around the world
gather the ropes and pulleys and lawsuits
to hoist humanity into this new era

there is no objective but clarity
a glimpse past the politics, the rulers,
the shopping malls, the TVs
that molded us into
this cultural configuration
a telescope to this moment
where tiny discoveries
blossom into
a desire to dig deeper
and fly

which is exactly what happens
as poem after poem lands
in my inbox
like rains after a drought
as I read
I realize
these youth are seeking
as I am
their truth
barefoot on the earth
and the earth
is setting
us free

Unplugged ~ 21

Another Day Alone

Today has no goal
unless breath is a goal

like yesterday
tomorrow
one moment
unfolding
the way it does

seamless stitches
into this colossal quilt
of choices

some call for one path
up the mountain

I call for many
offerings to the altar
found within me
inviting, burrowing
calm now
dark earth churning
mayhem
as close as ever
something else
appealing inside
quiet
asking me to walk
alone
for a while

let the questions
insist
like hail
outside
my open
window

Beautiful Shit Show

"Sheltering in place might be our best answer to climate change."
~ a septuagenarian friend

At the start of every new year
resolutions multiply
it's time to change
get rid of clutter
use the gym membership
exorcise the inner asshole
whose thumb tacks limitations
onto our reasoning

we want to change our lives
but do we?
routines stay the same
the TV shows, the work
the meals we eat
do we have the courage to throw
that stick of dynamite
confront the raw glare
of ourselves naked?

I'm not talking about
troublesome fat insurrections
angry liver skin or whatever else
we are supposed to hide in polite society
the tell-tell signs of choices
that make your average politician
give Michael Jackson
and Jane Fonda a runoff
for dollars allocated
to cosmetic expenditures

no I'm talking about the nitty
and the gritty
our actions lay bare
you know, like the crown

the planet is bowing to
genuflecting our rights
as if we had them in the first place
slumbering past the important parts of the Nuremberg code
like it's a nursery rhyme
a grim tale whose authors were only kidding
when they penned the part
about animals surviving the jab first
to make sure it never happens again

no we run nilly past the nitty
deep throating "science"
the corporate sponsored
government academia
that props up chemicals like glyphosate and PFAS
while fine scientists with eyebrows raised
self-silence to avoid the *vehement heresy*
that erodes corporate sponsored
government research funding
Galileo, how did you do it?
oh yeah, you rotted in jail
Copernicus what can we learn
from your tactics?

but this poem is about change
not the past
though I wonder if anyone remembers
science is about inquiry
don't even get me started on mouth panties

the digital faces like to say
the new normal, build back better
trust science
heralding the great reset
while we say silver linings
you know, the good things happening
while we're locked in our homes,
rebreathing co2, depriving ourselves of touch,
live music, and community
glued to trusted liars

cowering at conflicting data
dare it reveal the emperor's fabric
of this society

yes, I *have* become better ear friends
my garden adores me
I get to stay up all night
since all I have to do is wake up
and sit in front of a computer
it seems I have more time
but really it's just driving-time savings
I work just as much
probably more
what else is there to do?
watch the re-broadcasts?

I guess it's time for my revolutionary make-over
where I risk offending
the very people I love
with my conspicuous glee at
the ripe underbelly of all this newspeak

what else can I do but open my palms for change
rise up from my deep hole diving
speak, challenge
breathe in the tri-tone of silence
and intellectual disdain my utterances evoke

I will continue to masturbate
strive for clarity of intuition
pray for independent thinking
relinquish outcomes
embrace this beautiful shit show
write poems
like this
for anyone
who might be
listening

Dropper Full of Wake Up

I need some juice
some kind of love squeeze
perhaps with a splash of
clean water
to cleanse my palette
of the noise
cluttering its coherence

my heart beats a paintbrush
arcs wide
swaths of color
releasing rainbows
in every direction
its prism revealing
short straights
90 degree corners
of Pacman eating
his way through the minds

we just want to get back to normal
they all say
leaving me no choice
but to get on my knees
love every blade of grass
as if it were my own

this earth needs more of us
people willing to stand in the line
of hate and love anyway
tell the masters, the slaves
there is no victory when
people cower inside
throwing stones at neighbors
they once loved
perhaps they still love them

in this confusion
we are not so different
the have and the have nots
we are not to blame
history reminds us
the meek seek
silence in the prisons
others put them in
powers shackled
but never subdued

there is a star inside
each and every one of us
a star so bright
it shines despite the dull din
of the default dream
devised through
decisions deferred
even then
nobody can destroy
the essence of who we are

we are born into death
as if it is something to conquer

let it be known
I will not ride the dystopian train
I will not succumb to a new normal
I will not be
reset
repurposed
recycled
masked

my papers are within
fused to this flesh
like lightening
my only master

is the mystery waiting
behind my last exhale

until then
my eyes are open
like my heart
embracing community ways
body ways
touch ways

this star
expanding
in symmetry
our numbers
counting to one

Fly Om

I started sound healing school
it's been three days
already I'm wondering
if I can explode a fly
like a cancer cell

I imitate him
matching his buzzzzzzzzz
getting buzzed enough myself
to want to write this poem

he and his companions
—part of the *flytriarchy*—
have been tormenting me for weeks
a 7:30am alarm clock of figure eight copulatory rituals
casting incessant shadows
on the shri yantra pinned to my ceiling

instead of C and G wake up tuning
I am bombarded by white noise that isn't even white noise
a daemon overtone drone
perhaps an army deployed by the cabal
evil illuminati troupes sent to wrestle me
from the golden thread
tethering me to the delicious center
of this morning

as I sit with tea
journal in hand
wood fire emulating sunshine
every few words punctuated
by yet another fighter plane
blitzing my head
forcing me to give up this poem
and grab the swatter
zzzzzzzzzooooozzzzzzzoohhhzzzz

Big Daddy Patriarchy

Oh Daddy
you are so big and strong and sciencey
you make it less scary to be human

I'm so glad I am in the passenger seat
and you are manning the Space X Sputnik Moderna vehicle
hurtling through the collective nervous system of humanity
I can't imagine having to trust my innate anything

here are the car keys
to my sovereignty
the deed to my free will
the secret code to my lock screen

you can make all the calls from now on
as long as you promise to keep me alive
with your drive-through fast food,
iron-on
pharma

oh Daddy
I love how you move the mouths
of the good brothers and sisters
telling the vision over and over again
no matter what station I'm watching
they all say the same thing
so I don't have to bother with fact finding
all that boring research

and reading, oh god, reading
I am so much happier to watch
your snippets of perceived relevancy
read the pre-approved publications
cliff-noting the parts your virtuous
cancel-culturally trained thinkers

tell us are essential
it is so generous of you
to ladle me
all the labels

oh Daddy you are so good
and I'm such a bad girl
cause sometimes I falter
and think about fake news
I wormhole down bitchutes
follow the telegram signals
go off parlor rumbling
with the banned

please don't punish me Daddy
de-platform my lockdown social media existence
stop me from liking and ignoring the posts of the friends
you won't let me hang out with anymore

I don't mean to be curious
it's just sometimes I hear a faint voice that
says something that kinda makes sense
but I am trying to do better Daddy

plus I know it's okay because
sooner or later I'll get caught by one of your algorithmic
bread crumbs and find my way back to the safe pabulum
of your YouTube suggestions

Daddy, I know you staged wars,
paperclips and Tuskegees
just so I can sleep soundly at night
knowing you have all the power
I don't have to bother
my pretty little head with details

you can handcuff me to the bedposts
beat me down with foreclosures

unemployment and hospital wards
since you always do it for my own good
and the good of all

Daddy I'm right here
waiting for you in my bedroom
with your proverbial crotch
over my mouth
hoping you'll finally launch
this SS Goodship New Normal
let us go orange
so I can put on my little black dress
let you take me out
for General Tso Chicken
inside a real restaurant

view the "Big Daddy Patriarchy" poem movie here:
https://www.bmoreyou.net/big-daddy-patriarchy-a-video-poem

A Message To the Future

Sovereignty is my self love
so I sit tall in the tree of myself
stating you cannot cut me down
propaganda does not
sway the subterranean roots
of my sky funnel
I do not succumb
to experiments
nor do I stand quietly
while you ridicule me
and
the implications of life
science is an inquiry
few humans are willing to weld

go ahead, put your arm out
let them take what is yours to give
but do not expect my child
inner or otherwise
to participate
in your experiments

this ground and I say no
to your pangolin and bats
to your furin cleavage
to your prion disease
to your deep vein thrombosis
to your myocarditis
to your PCR PR

I rise up
illuminate the purpose of love

how many light bulbs will it take
to change humanity?

Science of Deep

Sometimes I wake up with myself
sometimes I don't
a willingness in this acceptance
like a Buddha who waits
patiently for me to catch up
with the moment
dwell now
unclouded by wishes
bearing this cavern of self
until *it* unfurls

a ray of amber sunflowers
appears in my right eye
full moon in the left
sunshine down the center

I have arrived
at the destiny of heat
facing purpose
with simple geometry
golden hands
planting heart
tilling sinew
mining equanimity
from the molten
earth
of myself

Do Butterflies Hug?
~ *for Time Magazine's cover man, September 2020*

I am not angry
I am righteous
I am not piteous
I am lifting myself
from the collective soma coma
perpetuated by numb media

I am not afraid
I am awake to the lies
willing to hold my head up
look directly into the sun
shining upon all of us

and ask you

who made you *the Science*
who told you to stop asking questions
who told you to judge
a persons right to somatic sovereignty
for the obfuscated safety of
relative risk reduction

who elected the man
with all the money
the man with his pockets in universities
and crisper technologies
the bureaucrat who told us there were no treatments
the man who got his pals
to publish papers
in *Nature* and *The Lancet*
carefully penned manipulations
that roared in like a lion
only to slither out in discreet paragraphs
the man with his hands in places
yet to be known

Unplugged ~ 35

hundreds of thousands of us dead
our own tax dollars
funding this disease of shady origins
suppressed for profit
just like the early treatments
that could have saved lives
not to mention medical licenses
and academic reputations

all so we could roll up our sleeves for beelzebub biology
the mice and monkeys and ferrets spared for once
we human beings deployed
for the advancement of bank accounts
and only god knows what else

are you ready to follow the FOIA trail of tears
or are you going to believe the man
who calls himself "Science"
the man with so much money
he could end homelessness in California

if Watergate happened today
you would not learn about it on Fox or CNN
if you did happen upon the tale of Nixon
and his break ins
you would be told not to believe it anyway

yes, Mr. Scott-Herron, I hear you loud and clear
the revolution
will not be televised

but it will
be apprehended

Anti Ode to a Mask

Oh farcical face panty
oh virtuous stifling smile suffocator
oh cataclysmic cloth of control
why are people still wearing you?
do they know you are implicated in
zits, teeth rot, bacterial pneumonia?

you are a chain link fence
keeping our consciousness from common sense
getting used to you means getting used
to less oxygen in our thoughts
you are the burka
the West never thought it would wear

you smell like a dusty dashboard
littered with pocket change
you look like a low budget sci-fi
running reruns on late night TV
you taste like yesterday's lunch from last week
excavated from the back of fridge
you feel like someone smothering me with a pillow
as they whisper *it is for your own good* into my ear
you sound like a muzzled mouth
vying for airtime at a cocktail party

thanks, yeah right, thanks mask
for the multitudinous, macabre hours
of jaw dropping
air stealing
excruciating
obligatory
tragicomedy

I hope the sea turtles like you
as much as
plastic straws

Pin Striping the Firmament

I don't want to see them
the incomprehensible hash marks
patterning the once blue
lined up in rows of six
at times
diagonally crossed
across atmosphere
coursing and spreading
all day long
sometimes low
right over my house

when did clouds start forming
perfect right angles
and X's over my head?
are the fallen angels
playing tic tac toe
with vapors
their game boards
stemming from metal tubes

tracks multiplying
transforming a pure day
into haze
in a matter of hours
exhilarating sunshine
into a grey
helplessness seeding
my heart

when I bring this up out loud
my cousin says
atmospheric scientists are identifying
new types clouds all the time
rendering my half century of sky watching
useless against the parapets of academia
but who funds their research?

he doesn't know

I am not the only one
who looks up with open lids
some of us talk about it in relieved tones
buoyed as each admission
loosens our straight jackets

stymied by the onslaught
we compare notes
in the summer
three days of pinstriping
followed by another dry thunder storm
our winter skies bent with hued halos
like rainbow slicks along a highway
of atmospheric rivers

we've never seen anything like it
relentless
today, yet again
jet butts for miles

so much so
they invaded my dream last night
this coast developed
into Cape Canaveral rocket pads
launching vertical 737s into the air
I do not consent
my dreams are mine
they tell me I must
do something
to face the neutering impact
floating down from the air above

which is why
I am putting so much love
into this poem
and am praying
it lands

Bespoke Suburbia
~ courtesy of the insistent voice inside

"Luxurious poison"
echoes between my ears
"aaaaaaaauuuuuuuuuuummmmmmm"
bellows down my heart
this alpha gamma voice
appearing in my center
says things like
"love yourself"
"stay positive"
"aluminum"

it gets me thinking
about all the ways my life succeeds
on the exertion of families
who make it so
men, women, children
who work hard
for our doodads and dothis's

aren't forever batteries the bomb?
I just love my personal fan
your electric car
and coke and pepsi—cheaper than water!
now that's a bargain
plus buck twenty-nine, metallic holographic duck tape
from the dollar store
I used to pay four dollars for that stuff
and that was the 90s!
it's the fix that keeps shit together

"NIMBY" pops into my head
all the shlep
the crap we're supposed to need
leave it to America
land of the free

to look the other way
while the disaster capitalized
CIA-overthrown
puppet government
third world
first world
shit hole country
citizens
slave their days away
so we beguiled humans
can bling bling
on the cheap
and shallow

A Lot of Hate to Love

A friend tells me that Jan 6
is worse than 911
that five deaths outweigh the 3000 from the towers
not to mention the slow or rapid decline
of countless first responders in the months, years, afterwards
to him, the assault on "democracy" is worse
because it came from inside

stay with me
I promise
while political in nature
I embrace no sides in this poem

next he says
I don't trust the democrats either
I know they are corrupt
but the republicans would be way worse
imagine if it were black people
who stormed the capital
imagine how many would be dead
or in jail

hmmm…last I read Americans of "color" are incarcerated
at roughly five times the rate of whites
so they are already screwed
besides, who is to say no
BIPOCs joined the merry band of "constitutionalists"
"storming the capital" for election rigging?
from the pictures I saw, January 6
like the race riots of the 1960s
was mixed
but I digress

yep, the US establishment has been barreling non-whites
for hundreds of years
those who know it
teach their young boys to say "yassir"

keep their hands visible
in all interactions
lest they are shot for driving while dark
or making eye contact with the banker's wife

he's right, if the hoodie kids who hit
Minneapolis or Portland or Seattle or Los Angeles
were to storm the capital
it would have been a shit show

let's visit the Oakland of today
inner city gangs
drawn to potent gangtsa rap role models
taking the streets
in ways the two parties clink champagne gasses over
disaster capitalism, insider-fueled power pulling
designed to produce drug turf fantasy realities
big booty, side shows
gold-grilled neighborhood splattering glorifications
funded by the very government we fund
which is to say
us

yep, we are all angry for our own reasons
perhaps mostly because of the erosion
of our inalienable rights
because even white folks
are finally beginning to understand
that being able to choose among 40 sugar cereals
or a couple of dozen drive-thrus
is not really freedom

free-range slaves, all of us
led to embrace the idea
that some of us can have it a little better
than others
in our open air prisions

it's folly to think that any Party wants the best for us
they don't have our back

they have their funders backs
if those pet regime projects nurture us
bully for us
if not, SOL sucka

it is like pharma side effects—
sometimes our asshole leaks
sometimes we get a hard on—
we think it is our choice

the system's been trading us
like cheap coins
rubber stamping our ideals
back and forth for centuries
offering us celluloid fantasies
to make it all more palatable
in 1 hour and 50 minute increments

how to stop it?
give up self-prescribing
ourselves into
media manufactured factions
like insidious happy hate pills

usually the Democrats are disgusting
typically the Republicans are abhorrent
together they push the sandbox teeter totter
up and down, up and down
four legs funded by the system
making overcredulous humans
responsible for climate change
inflation
recession
as the industrial complex rakes in record profits

the Democrats fought to keep slavery!
the Republicans fought to end abortion!
the Democrats want to force vaccinate the planet
the Republicans want your kids to keep their birth gender
yet they both vote

to suspend government
hide money transfer between agencies
hire 87,000 new IRS agents
they both vote to send more billions to war
while homelessness in America hits record numbers
they both decide how our money disappears

how would the Boston Tea Party appear on Facebook?
do you think the talking heads
would have cancelled the colonists
for disrespecting King George and his redcoat minions?
perhaps you might look toward
ex-*New York Times* darling Alex Berenson
to ride back into the spotlight on his reinstated X-Twitter horse
all plumped up by his undisclosed legal settlement
like Paul Revere blue checking
his revolutionary shouting
censorship is here
censorship is here
inviting everyone into the gallery
of shadow banning and suiciding
deep into the underground bowels
of modern day insurrection
so perhaps we can pull our heads out
of the propaganda toilet
get back to making a stand, right here
in our hearts, homes, neighborhoods
cross the purple bridge
arms around each other
clearing the hate crust from of our eyes
laughing and crying about how asleep we have been
getting on with it

love is the only insurrection
worthy of air time

He-ART-I-Facts

Even though the media dickles appear
to have taken over the collective dinner hour
a growing forest of ourselves
like impish elves
embrace herd impunity
some in long stretches of deep and silent
others braving the virtue parade
somehow shielded from the double masks
of the woke asleep

Teflon I tell you, we should be made of PFAS
who knows, maybe we will be soon
hurling science and not science at each other
destroying brand new data
in collective control group conjabs
no long term effects worry now
no short term injury nonsense to think about
let's shove those adverse effects
back into the drawer
vaccinate the kiddos
just do it say the leaders
who sponsored this virus
who bragged in public
that their test can't differentiate
between the flu and the thing
anyway

huh? is anyone paying attention?
why aren't we protesting every instance
of brave new world speak
like that woman asking why
the protected need
to be protected from the unprotected
by forcing the unprotected
to use the protection that didn't
protect the protected in the first place

the cognitive dissonance rising
like a sloshed sun hammering down
doors of the cellar

people quitting, retiring early, getting fired
giving up the toiling fruits of their best years
starting positions on the team
medical licenses
badges and boots
indignities paraded across the press
like evening death tallies in our contemporary hunger games
experts chomping and growling and wennie waggling
at selfish bloodstained people like me

last I checked, we were not born to tell each other what to do
we are not here to bow down to hypocrites
comply our way out of Big Brotherdom
but divided we do
which is why they want you to blame everything
on the **homicidal, flat-earth-heralding**
climate-change-denying, racist, communist
tinfoil-hat-head, trump-supporting, FJB-cheering
conspiracy-theorist, disease-spreaders

the notice from my healthcare provider
promises not to discriminate
based on race, religion, gender identity
sex, disability, age, sexual orientation, marital status
political beliefs, nationality or economic position
no mention of vaccine status

yeah right
get to the back
of the bus
you murderer

The Big Lie

~ Definition: A lie so big, so outrageous, that most people cannot conceive of someone being audacious enough to tell it

The grand and shoddy machine
under cover of the Hollywood curtain
seeks to ban
ban anyone onto the big eye lie
horrified by we, the freedom of voice
mouths gaped open over the newspaper
masked shut on the sidewalk
racing minds huddled and howled
under the gales of fat men
laughing and counting
everyone trying to make sense of the story
stretched out before them
like Pinocchio's nose

it is inconceivable that anyone
regulatory or otherwise
would serve themselves
at the expense
of so many

but look
out there, out here
in the burn barrel pages of time,
up high on the hill
in the musky shadows
is history's gullibility guillotine

terrified of talkback
we accept the drunk dad
coming home with a handful of fists
slamming them into our wabbling walls
don't ask any questions
no spooky speculations
never defy the almighty truth legislators

no no no
stay quiet
until your mouth bleeds
under the weight of teeth
struggling to scream
STOP

what is the agenda
destitution? death?
social credit system?
Apple robs Chinese iPhones of their airdrop function
during a banking protest
Wechat, all your banking, social, navigational, recreational
organizational, professional, sexual, governmental identity needs
in one simple app
put a chip in your brain
and you'll never have to look at that subway map again
or read a menu, just scan the QR code
with your very own iris reader
extra bonus, AR goggles, no longer necessary
plus you will love your 15 minute city
never mind the fines for leaving it too many times this year
you won't be able to afford gas anyway
we are going to take your car
cause you are causing
the climate to change
all you tiny people
under the weight of our bombs
manufacturing methods, cobalt mining

if only it was that obvious
do you think dystopia can happen here?
check your shoes
for explosives
take off your belt
swab your nose
sorry mam, our bathrooms are closed for customers

ever wonder why
we are so easy to cow and coral?

Unplugged ~ 49

it is because we humans
are, for the most part, good
yep I said it, the big generalization
in lockstep with the big lie
we care about each other
want to do what is right
even if the people who tell us to do it
are bad daddy narcissistic psychopaths
preying on our unresolved traumas

pandemic or catastrophe capitalism
a sneaky virus who preferred
family owned business over chain outlets
forced you stay 6 feet apart
until you boarded the plane
let you take your masks off at the table
coerced you into taking a shoddy shot

it is a psyop of monarch mockingbirds
yet no matter how many master disaster chains are rattled
billions spent on PR control campaigns
statistics skewed by empirical data delivery
they don't have the power
in their numbers
we know it in the spin of our spines
we have words
the power of vibration

so let's talk
talk loud
talk tall
talk proud
speak through the flim flam film sham
squawk aloud
stop thinking about consequences
the only way forward
is to be forward

we are in this
we are all there is

has been
ever can be
it takes us
shining the vibration
into the void
outloud
loud
saying no
from the
mycelial roots
reaching up
like the star souls
of soil
we are

Anti Ode to Mr Global

Oh insidious totalitarian polyp of time
oh blue-pilled illusion of free will
oh brain-numbing manipulative molesting bad dad

why don't people recognize your CIA tricks
and CGI newsreels?
how does it feel to know that some of us are onto you?

have you ever imagined being forced to share
your meager trillions with the rest of us?
how do you close your eyes at night
with so much incestuous ghoully gore
and bankruptcy on your hands?
are you haunted by paper-clipped ghosts
and lorazapamed grandparents?

you are small businesses
dying in the shadows of over-hyped box stores
junkies sleeping and shitting on San Francisco sidewalks
families of six eating cold instant noodles in their cars
dusty farms praying for sanctioned fertilizers

you are a tunnel
trying to turn off any hope
for light at the end
you are rabid, health annihilating pollution
daring to pass yourself off as our fault
you are chain grocers
peddling processed chemicals
as if it was food
you are choices
we never know to make

you smell like climate changing aluminum
and deet around the campfire
you look like 600 private jets gathering
to determine the fate of the proletariat

you taste like a bowl full of glyphosate
sprinkled with microplastics
you feel like a warty dinosaur
insisting on the extinction of humanity

you sound like broadcasters
parroting fear into the hearts
of the lonely and gullible

you pilfer the dreams of the many
and dole them out to your buddies in blackmail

thank you, yes thank you
Mr Globalony
your jig is up
as you finally become
so bloody obvious
to anyone
who dares
lift the lid
off the trashcan
of your
dying
lying
legacy

HoHoHum

~for the ghost of Christmas past

It's the wonderful time of year
hot coco, velvet stockings
red green tinsel
reindeer lounge wear
matching rudolph hats
hark ye merry merchant
sugar amped box sale
Hallmark Holiday
hurting my teeth

fantasy smiles
trying to make whatever the F
is happening here
on Earth, circa pandemicky December
taste like a plate of homemade cookies
waiting patiently by fireplace
instead of high fructose coal lump
punches in the gut

I searched Netflix for "Covid-19 Christmas"
but nothing came up, no masks
no nose probing to attend the tree lighting
no hazmat suit Santas
with triple jabbed kiddos
perched on his lap
not one hospital ward among them
where were the sugarplum ballerinas checking for vax cards?
the AI recognition software stopping the Girl Scout moms
from taking the Juniors to see the Rockettes?
somehow the Hollywood nutcrackers
managed to elude
the dystopian, FTX fairytale
once again

I don't blame the producers
for shadow banning the X-mas hellscape
that is this season's joy
for wanting us to forget
the chimney is crammed with disinvited family members
Klaus's naughty list growing longer
with every missed booster
it makes me want to ginch-bomb a Zoom room
and carol
how about you?
do you feel it too?
come on, join me
in some holiday cheer-down
sing it with me,
one, two, and a one two three...

They know that Santa's in his mask;
He's loaded lots of tests and needles
on his sleigh.
And ev'ry mother's
child is gonna cry
to see that Pfizer really knows how to lie

In the New Year

In the New Year
things will be different.
no one will lose their job
their ability to enter a movie theater
their family's respect
it will be all day red pills
with brand new solar plexi
wrap-around arms
actual dancing

the ideas of last year will have
vibrated out of earshot
gone gone gone
like a terrible cold
whose tissues
are uniformly banned
in a hazmat can

while back here
on planet right now
we'll be cleaning out
the pockets
of wrinkled CEOs
hiding in trillion dollar stacks
vacuuming Senate seats
rounding up big tech cockroaches
sweeping the floors of justice

right here, in the New Year
our skies will stop
playing SOS
and our children
will finally
be safe

www.TV

Why we watch TV
we watch TV
so we don't think
other than the prescribed
thoughts that come to us
through the box

we hear ourselves
falling in love, out of love
stealing, cheating, maiming, killing
dying of disease
blowing up bad guys
losing a few good ones
exploring galaxies far far away

we succeed and fail
wake up in the morning
talk about it with our lovers, our friends
at school, at work

it is an institutional past time
a comforting straight jacket
we willingly don
to pass the moments
relax between clocking in
serial shows and news hours
spreading
into days
into months
into ideas
we claim as our own

I was programmed
by *Barney, Happy Days, Brady Bunch*
that was my generation X
others made *Sex in the City*
Friends fell for *Seinfeld*

I even dated a Kramer once
It's Always Sunny in Philadelphia
he used to say

my youngest poets want to write
about *Pokeman Baby Shark Spongebob
Minecraft Fortnight*
the last two aren't really shows
but they captivate stanzas just the same
I remember when it was *Grand Theft Auto*
I don't hear about that anymore
now it is a phone game where teenagers
push buildings into holes
rack up points
based upon the number
of people who die
when the skyscraper disappears
into the ground
like Tower 7

it's a *Tiger King* in the *Ozarks
House of Cards*
the stakes keep mounting
more money is printed
planes spray sulfate aerosol particles
in the dark of night
to combat global warming
railroad companies detonate dioxin bombs
so they can get their trains back on the tracks
politicians pretend to fight
while they collect the lobbyist dole
Silicon Valley banks
sink under the weight of their executive withdrawals

but don't worry
tax payers will bail out
the corpulent cats
once again
the gap widening
between the haves

and the wish-they-hads
as the *Twilight Zone*
of *Twilight* vampires
begets the same
Game of Thrones
Villains and Victors
Sex, Lies and Power Play vortices

while we the serfs
watch the tsunamis, fires, earthquakes
unfold on our devices
as if the traumas they play out
through our vision
are occurring within our own bodies

basing lives around
the voices we prefer
like we are celebrated stars
the lucky teenager
banging the *Weed* MILF
the so-so guy suavely picking up
the only *10* in the bar
posting our head shots on Insta
the *People Magazine* for commoners
used to teach the AI
to eliminate our free will

playing out their script
exactly as predicted
for our own academy awards
pork chops and applesauce
like Jan and Peter
Kanye and Drake
we tweet insults at each other
cheat on our partners
loot the corner store
hell, maybe even shoot up a church
some how think
we are doing something
when really

we are sleeping
sleeping soundly
under the pillow of programming
spells cast
like dreams
to keep us drugged
unconcerned
with our own ideas

saucer-eyed zombies
acquiescing in the blue light
black mirror
one and zero
diode flashing
wand
made of
holly wood

can you
turn it off?

Unzip the Mind Bag

M for money
I for ideology
C for coercion
E for ego
what does that spell?
that's right
plural of mouse
a bevy of rodents
sneaking around
the spy world
figuring out new ways
to focus the plebes
pandemic
famine
war
the horses
of man's inflicted horrors
MK Ultra
butterfly monarch
paperclip
mockingbird
scarcity narcissism
corporate cult
pharma ashrams
everyone is a nazi
when communist fingerpointing
we are all villains
because everyone else is stupid
robbing ourselves from the heart
giving into the head
kill the oppressor
destroy ourselves
in the 8th sphere meta desert
statistics replace creativity
division trumps time
threats upon threats
cracks of lightening

piercing the porno
thundering screams
along the edges of existence
bars of belief prison
close in
as brand name illusions
invert our identity
divert our dignity
subvert our future
greatness anywhere but here
the possibility of anything but now
indoctrinate, indoctrinate
trauma bonding
ritualized events
disaster capitalism
economic hit men
charging the furniture
with sinking dollars
rearranging the living room
till there is no war to end all wars
just a way to transfigure
the configuration
of a psychopathic non-sentient world

man is not mechanical
man is flesh
flesh is word
language is ours

it is time
to talk
to love

employ
the blockchains
of ourselves

The First Amendment in the time of Cancelling

~ *Sticks and stones may break your bones, but words will never…*

When did words become seditious
dangerous enough to label their utterer
a domestic terrorist
kind-hearted people afraid to speak
least they inflict perceived bodily harm
with awkwardly placed pronouns
about their confusion over motherhood
micro agressions
hiding in every breath

anyone bleeding yet?

or their number crunching realization
that a person was only considered vaccinated
14-days after a second shot
daring to ask how many "un-vaxxed" deaths
were just waiting for their days to countdown

are you cowering under my blows?

or wondering aloud why SBF post FTX meltdown
flew from The Bahamas to NYC
for a keynote hang with Zelensky, the US Treasury Secretary
prezes of TikTok, Amazon and other bigs
at an exclusive NYT event
cameras rolling when the joker-faced SBF
quipped "it has been a rough month"
as the dressed-to-impress audience belly laughed
yep, a collective three letter guffaw
SOL retiree suckas
who trusted the guy the fact checkers said
was most trusted crypto guy
whom *Fortune* dubbed "the New Warren Buffett"

oh gosh, did someone just die
under the weight of my loose tongue knives?

free speech insurgences
swinging from the orange jumpsuit
Eppstein wore to his hanging
the official story we voluntarily zip ourselves into
every time we do a goddamn web search

it's killing me!

is honesty a mental illness?
do we become threats to ourselves
if we question
the line the alphabet agencies draw in the sand?
one mask, two mask, three mask, N95
ADL, WEF, DNC, GOP, YE
pre-bunking
moonshots raking in redirected searches
military industrial corporate confounding pollution
cloaked in climate change

hell, in five minutes, the SR-72 Skunk Works
is jizzing all over YouTube with—
pollutes more than any measly nitrogen
some poor Dutch farmer spreads on his crops in his lifetime!

it's redistribution of land I tell you
an effort to further centralize our food supply
eat zee bugs, eat zee bugs
oh did I smite someone else?

where's my mouth tape
lock up my tongue
elections
pharma
sudden adult death syndrome
UFOs UAPs
gender reassignment surgery
parental rights

reproductive rights
child trafficking
US borders
loan forgiveness
the president
which president
all presidents!
science
abject objectivity
debate in arrears
death to inquiry
free will traded for safety
perhaps the ability
to pay the mortgage
cover the kids college
learn something new

yep Yale
Yale University
forces its germy students
to get the only-tested-on-8-mice-bivalent shot
if they want to learn how to rule the world
but the faculty and staff
they can skip it

opps? did I just inflict more terror?

private jets and yachts exempt from carbon credits
owners so important
they can expend my entire life's carbon emission in
a single cross Atlantic flight

okay, I'll drop the box cutters…

yet if I post this crap online
somehow garner "followers"
the pickpocketing, thought police
can freeze my accounts and seize my assets
for DVE -- **that's** domestic violent extremism
as if America is Central America

I think maybe it is
CIA tactics perfected on the third world
coming home to roost

yay! we are all so happy
with sports and weekends
making our house beautiful with cheap shit from Cosco
we go along to get along

unaware that our brothers and sisters in voice
walk among us
like suicide DVEs
willing to risk pre-crime
for the sanctity of
a free life
your life
my life
everybody's life

Vanilla ISIS
is not an ice cream flavor
look it up
just not on Google

Dear Prussian Prudence

School is a cult of Control
I say
a place where white walls
make right angles
square desks
and **quadrangular** *whiteboards*
lay out pre-programmed ideas
institutionalizing
thought in stultifying proportions

the principal looks at me
and says nothing
I take it to mean
he doesn't want me to stop
so I continue

school is a brain bin
packing kids
into bygones
but telling them
it's their future
as if consensus science
was about innovation
all the while
bureaucratic strings get pulled
from sickle circles above
and even though we see it
none of us seem
to want to stop
the machine gunning
for us all

he appears done with listening
so I lean back and breathe
giving him room to say
something
but all I hear is rumbling

rumbling
that persistent rumbling
rumble littering our sky
with rumbling again

we both look up
say nothing
say nothing about
the rumbling remains
X and why axis vapors
sectioning
criss-crossing
obscuring the sky
above the campus
in their stratospheric
aerosol
injection
lines

in our silence
we acknowledge
we also sat in rows
took tests
with answer boxes
ate processed food
from rectangle trays
repeated whatever
we were taught
to get ahead

Willful Ignorance

Intolerance in
the guise of tolerance
dereliction of duty
of humanity
compassion corrupted
empathy subverted
double dealing artists
helping the system
close our inquisitive mouths
asphyxiating hope
drowning dreams of subversion
in acronyms
in commercials
in print

tyranny is incremental
trigger is a trigger word
I am triggered by
liberals
republicans
woke
anti-woke
I am marooned
in a sea of beliefs
adrift amid attacks on
women
men
gays
trans
TERFs
comedy
Israelis
Palestinians
opinions

a man won the Hersey's Woman of the World Award
all I got was poetic indigestion

Do You Believe?

Do you believe
in using children as mice?
do you believe
in DARPA?
do you believe
the future of humanity
is deeper within us
than we've been shown?
do you believe condensation from airplanes
causes the sun to disappear?
do you believe the people who died suddenly
just died suddenly like babies die suddenly
because something in our biology
is flawed?
do you believe
humans are flawed?
do you believe you are flawed?
that it is our nature to control and enslave one another?
do you lord over others?
is this your way of life?
is this your nature?
is this what you believe?
do you want to see your children grow up?
do you want to see them run through grass, snow and ocean
witness them experience themselves
as creatures of earth?
what it feels like to have free will over their own body?
free will that harms no bone
free will that is bigger than a mandate
or some universal biometric trigger

free will
free will
free will
something our ancestors secured

don't close your eyes

stay awake
as the walls inch closer

pay no attention to the fucking
sucking eating shopping gossiping
stop working, too much working

stop working dreams you don't believe in
measuring life as commerce
retail commitments
trap free range slaves
into believing in freedom
unaware that every molecule of the motor
works to wrestle away sovereignty

stand up for love
with love
audit discrepancies
query complicity
trim the trespassers
touch the toroidal vortex
reflected in the illuminated heart of the whole
chestahedron monatomic gold flashes
radiate around the closed wall shell of bastard creations
dissolve crisper genes
man-made biology

innate selves reflecting
unity field biology
the ocean
under our skin
expressing
the present
breathing
beyond
belief
winning within us
if we dare

Drink a Little Poison or Go Thirsty

Two tall canteens of well water gone
still dancing
no plastic bottles left to buy
forcing the choice
city water or dry mouth?

poisoning undermines dehydration
I think as I hit the tap
the yummy nasty chemmie water softener taste
reminds me of why I hated water as a kid

since this water
meets federal standards
it contains eight contaminants that exceed
scientific health concerns
can you pronounce them?
I can pronounce the first one
fluoride…
but what about
bromodichloromethane
bromoform chloroform
dibromoacetic acid
dibromochloromethane haloacetic acids (HAA5)
trihalomethanes (TTHMs)
surprise surprise
every one of these extra ingredients
is implicated in cancer

annoyed and cornered
I remind myself of my tools
and as the fluoro-chloro-dibro-halo-tri-methane stream
travels through my electro-magnetic field
I think, yes, yes I can restructure you water
turn you into hexa meta tetra sophistication
something geometric and beautiful
worth drinking for sure

as I drink
I pray
then water says
I know myself
water says
find me
I belong to you
I am you
all the understandings
you thought impossible
drink me
flow with me
follow me
into the heart of your electro-liquid center
speak truth for water
speak truth for all waters
coursing into oceans
all oceans
reach in, reach up
inside yourself
earth
atmosphere
milky way
keep reaching
then stop
find yourself

swallow

Start Making Sense

The saying is everywhere these days
"the truth shall set you free"
the pithy cliche from the book
saving and enslaving so many
what does it mean
what's truth?
what's free?
how much is it?
can you think about
the skeletons haunting the ashes
of the recent years
without suicide?
do you have the stomach
to watch without fear?
can you transform horror
into a dream
of peace?

whether we like it or not
there is nothing left to do
but love
real love, true love, tough love
goodbye co-dependent
bow down low love
adios groveling closed eyes, taped-mouth
false-kindness love
sayonara sycophant suckubusses love

we gotta love fierce
love independent
love the chaos
taking balance away
so we can love
imbalance
back into balance
again

Ode to Emotional Intelligence

Oh ever-adapting heart
oh gnat-swatting, problem-solving, foe-erasing wit
oh fast-talking, perpetually-smiling mouth that keeps me employed
do you know the stars pour ideas into my head?
why doesn't everyone let you run their lives?
have you ever thought about creating a franchise?
I think you could help us build a more well-rounded species

you are 8 billion tiny bulbs of love trying to find each other
amid the dark forests of misplaced culture
you sing louder than cicadas in the summertime
yet in a frequency so fine
it takes some humans lifetimes to hear, if at all
you are an open window
yet stronger than any wall

you smell like cinnamon apples baking in grandma's oven
you look like people holding hands in the streets
you taste like sunshine after weeks of rain
you feel like decades of soaring deep beneath the sea
you sound like the trees when I remember to listen

thank you for never giving up on me
thank you for knowing
I will never give up on you

Tea and Tango
~ for Point Arena

Whether we say so or not
this place is paradise
a vast expanse
inside the cubicles of each heart
a boundless vista
of discovery circulating
the progression of orbs
beating breathing being

it challenges us to seek
something bigger
than confused rules
unbalanced checks
six foot distances
gossip

what is fear but a skipped beat
a sucking in of clatter
the daily newsfeed

the terroir of this town, like all towns
enjoins us to listen
reflect the impact of words
lift up poems
the size of oceans
toss aside derision
get into the middle
of the water
look around
swim
in the current of now
as it flows
towards our elected future

so many of us here
waiting for someone to say something
to inhale again
to laugh and speak
me too
stretching out hands
for hugs, for strength
for community

reclaim what it is
dance the same song
frolic in fresh air
grass especially green
jack boots in the closet
growing dusty, moth eaten
once again

history does not have to repeat
it doesn't even want to
we have the power
to say no to terror
say yes to each other

we have the power
to stop fighting
a war of our own making
a war designed to divide and destroy us
a war that is not ours
a war nobody will ever win

together our tongues
create change
discover love
in unfamiliar landscapes
recast the dye
sculpt a limitless path
mirroring the wild beauty
of this hearth
on earth

Love Is My Currency

In these inflationary times
everyone wants to extend
their six dollar gallon of gas
maybe discover a thrift store
wait in line for another free shot
but what if the hamster wheel
stops turning for cheese and diet coke
what if it rolls itself right off a cliff
crashes into the deep blue ocean
would you care too much
or not care at all?

it's like this now
all black and white
the sky the only gray
in our confirmationally biased lives
our attention running this way and that
as our leaders kick the can
into the abyss with one foot
dig our graves with the other

cynical, did you just call me cynical?
the exact opposite
a cynical person would not bother
with all this nonsense
she'd be living in Mexico or Miami
with a young coconut in one hand
a smiling man in the other

I understand what exchange means
it is creation
it is freedom
it is the willingness to open my mouth
risk everything
I will speak as the cerulean above is eclipsed behind

mysterious exhaust lines
I will open my mouth as our leaders attempt to grant
unprecedented powers
to unelected bureaucrats
inject highly marketable children
without their parents consent
I will talk as California takes away
a doctors right to practice medicine
if it does not fall lockstep
with the "don't question me I'm science" guy

my voice has value
it has love
so does yours
words are a currency of change
of growth
the courage we gather
from these sovereign mouths
joined in mutual willingness
is much more potent than Wikipedia
or the ministry of disinformation

I will risk being wrong
so you can help
me understand
we are not so different
gray is good
when it isn't spewing
into a river
or raging
from a cigarette
in my face

I will not cancel you
please don't
cancel me
teach me
so collectively we
stay free

Unplugged ~ 79

Peace Be Kind

~ Think Peace and Be Kind, 2022 Point Arena Parade theme

"Think peace and be kind"
a clarion call for this time
of unprecedented endurance
the world both smaller and bigger
as we lift the goggles
to repel the frequency skirmishes
sundry manipulations
designed to thwart our coming together

these rays of ourselves
are meant to shine
illuminate the sun path
making us impossible to stop
no matter how fierce the storm
our epicenter knows how to survive
when we moor our minds to sky
fasten our feet to earth
knowing we all want
the same thing
even if we name it
something different

peace as the sunset affirms
another day of belonging
love as it rises before our eyes
in the light of morning
stability as the moon dances
above the tallest tree

we are a wave vaster than
any division
any particle
a mural of rainbow proportions
stretching as far as our imagination

80 ~ Dystopia

our tenderness
fortifies our strength

we are a quartz megaphone
roiling and ringing
within the cauldron
of this human vulnerability

we must embrace tolerance
the science of heart math
if we wish to survive
into the intimacy
of telling our visions
spelling out
our compassion
grasping that there is
no sweetness
when hearts have hate
no melody
when mouths spill anger
no sustenance
when intolerance fogs our head
no rest when we go to sleep
unsettled

here we are parading again
rising up within ourselves
gathering like a solar system
extending its concentric revolutions
into a cosmos of understanding

it has been a long two years
since we gathered like this
our celebrations shifting
we have all lost something
it is our common denominator
our initiation to empathy
we have what it takes
we know it

here we are
still alive
opening ourselves to the world
we nearly let go
hugging each other
inviting friends back to our tables

this tender community
realizing the only way out
is through
looking into the horror
recognizing its beauty

the age of Aquarius
has dawned
now it is up
to us
to live it

Forgiveness 101

Sometimes life kicks
you in the guzzler
takes your love and twists
it into an origami monster
stomping circles
in the attic
wrecking havoc on the very floorboards
of the foundation
the mind is a terrible thing
to piss off

there is nowhere to run
but to the heart
it does not want to hold grudges
instead it offers armfuls of daisies
candlelit courtyards in moonlight
it says "how can I help"
"do you need anything"
and "gosh some people
must be very unhappy"

why else would they sic the county on you
call you "stupid" during a board meeting
determine you are unfit for the costume job
with the social activist musical comedic political theater company
you've had for over 20 years
because you did not get the shot
that still doesn't work

change is hard
but tyrannical change is torment
not the expected torture
but the relentless wonder
over the bureaucratic betrayers
their kindergarten tattle tactics
why nobody spoke directly to me
why they chose to embrace
the institutions they spent decades parodying

why I was iced out of my own world
labelled a *flat earther*

without intention
my groove deepens
making the step
out of righteousness
steeper than necessary

revenge is sweet
but forgiveness is death-defying

the latter
the only
chance
for survival

Seeing Abundance

There is enough food
enough water
air
tolerance
hands to hold
children to teach

the future is alive
with smiling eyes
safe hearts
strong bodies

woes of the mind
a distant shadow
of what was needed
to bring us here

Wake the Bear

California sings stories
cries fires and homelessness
hungers for liberty, for immigrants
wears unicorn onsies and REI
glitters her sidewalks with stars
ubiquitous sunshine and bottomless sauv blanc
framing her perception

she thinks she's better than the other 49
she knows it
maybe I do too

she is my refuge
she is my prison
my best friend
my soul murderer

I'll never leave her
my co-dependent, gas-lit heart
won't let me

she knows it
demands I stay
forget Tennessee, New Hampshire, Idaho
other states appearing to unhook
from the fairy tale

from her hospital bed
she winks through masked gasps
and I understand
she wants me to poke the bear
back to freedom
independence
tolerance

liberate the sleeping compassionate
from their smothering pillows of pharmedia

all the while
her leaders run marathons
in my mind
exhausting me
with clever words
building inspectors
tax codes
vaccine mandates

yet I need this land
her
as life needs water
a sweatshop needs children
her heirloom bread shops and yoga pants
her arrogance
her Birkenstock footprints
marking the sands of time

her persistent ocean
beside me
her never tiring redwoods
her amanita muscaria wrapping paper
her absconded Woodstock ideals
clogged with empty pipe dreams

she is the drain of the west
that masquerades as its faucet
distorting our visions
with bougie tasting rooms
Hollywood agitprop
Vandenburg sky shows

Silicon sitcoms
augmenting our desires
their googlie-eyed AI fantasies laced
with immortality
and errant brain chips
striving to extend the cognitive failing
of ancient politicos

I won't turn away

Unplugged ~ 87

Tolerance is Bliss

We abide this ledge of cosmos
the micro macro
or macro micro
of ocean roar and redwood

we are a tall order
under remote lens
confronted every day by the sheer beauty of ourselves
fox cries echoing through the wind
a mountain lion darting along the perimeter
hummingbird showering beneath garden sprayer

we are the whales, hawks, bear and deer
the gathering squirrels and naked ladies
of day time
the owls and howls of night
we shoot like stars
rest like ravens

we pulse land and water
through our bodies
individually and collectively
we resonate
as we deliver apples
fix the leak
raise the barn
speed towards the hospital

alone and together
we mirror the whole
weeks of solitude reflected in ocean wave
cumulative understanding

we are this earth
and this earth is holding us up
even when we grind our teeth and forget to breathe
the screen inside our mind is not a goal

88 ~ Dystopia

inhaling is a goal
exhaling its reward
one moment unfolding the way it does
seamless stitches
into this spell of choices

some call it *about time*
I call it a circle
no end, no beginning
just one continuous flow
offerings from turquoise sea
stretched out below
inviting, diving
cavernous and calm
churning tumult, a world away

this inner tending is our green peace
self care activism
revealing vast constellations and wild animals within

we are waking up
walking along the deep steep
juking and dodging the questions
as they insist like rain
into a thirsty mouth

soon we will realize
we are the answers
as we find new ways
to watch, learn, listen, share
touch our double helix
reclaim it
with our lives

View the "Tolerence is Bliss" poem movie here:
https://www.bmoreyou.net/tolerance-is-bliss-a-video-poem

You Are You

Today, more than ever
I am Jesus
laying prayers on the divided
so we can see we are
one humanity
not two halves
pretending to be whole

I am Buddha
sitting calmly amid chaos
trees swaying
silence into my belly
out into the world

this moment, just like always
I am Rumi
spinning love songs with breath
dancing god into limbs
so we can walk with awe

I am Quan Yin
opening the lotus of time
to reveal the sunrise of humanity
as we claim our sovereignty

tonight, my heart on the edge of sky
I am God
bowed deep in the marrow
of this glorious earth
listening to moonlight whisper
sweet everythings into my pen
even if I don't quite believe
what I'm hearing

but owls agree

and night insects and foxes
shooting stars reveal secrets
we already know
if we listen

right now
more than ever
the deep galaxies of us
pulse with an invitation
to swim in waves of humanity
not there, but here
right here, in this skin
our skin, human skin
human bodies
twist strands
into DNA
of our making
love it
feel it
be it

beauty big and small
wander infinity
explore emptiness
on foot and in dreams

this is the life we have
furled forth in cosmic communities
now is why we are here

vastness
ready for helm
we are the sacred symbol
tetrahedrons
spinning open
the flower of life

View the "You Are You" poem movie here: https://www.bmoreyou.net/you-are-you-a-video-poem

Please Talk Back

I do not recognize myself
I don't even answer
to my name
unless you say it
over and over

by then
it is nonsense
I can't put
my tongue on

who am I
a voice in a head
a daughter
a poet
your friend

ideas land
take off
just as quickly

pain does that
slips into the marrow
and throbs
yowling
notice me
notice me

change

About the author

Longtime resident of California's Mendocino Coast and living off-grid since 1999, Blake More is a healing artist with many creative voices and expressions. Often called a "renaissance woman", Blake's expressions range from poetry, multi-media arts & video to music, holistic gardening, and sound healing. Poet Laureate of Point Arena, CA, she hosts the monthly Third Thursday Poetry & Jazz event and two radio shows: Be More Now on KZYX FM Mendocino County Public Broadcasting and Cartwheels on the Sky on KGUA FM Gualala. She also works with California Poets in the Schools and the California Arts Council to deliver creative arts instruction in K-12 classrooms around Mendocino County. As a poet and dancer Blake has performed in Tokyo, Amsterdam, New York, Los Angeles and throughout the SF Bay area. She has written two non-fiction books, one fiction book, and five books of poetry, and her freelance writings have appeared in dozens of magazines, including *Yoga Journal, Utne Reader* & *Tokyo Time Out*. For an extensive list and exploration of Blake More's creative healing world please visit her website: bmoreyou.net.

What others are saying

If honesty is a mental illness, the poetry in Blake More's *dystopia unplugged - please talk back* is crazy wisdom. Full of earthy gravitas, Blake's poetry is tethered to the stars. Her feral sovereignty is a soulful mirror for our unasked questions.

~ Fred Mitouer, Ph.D., Author *Wounds into Blessings* and *Dragons' Breath Theater* "only boring people get bored", "repeated whatever/we were taught/to get ahead", "the ocean/under our skin/expressing/the present/breathing beyond belief/winning within us/if we dare," Blake More trusts her heart and writes from her gut without thought of apology or shadow of fear —if this isn't a vivid explosion of what it means to say what you feel, I don't know what is.

> ~ Martin Hickel, Marin Poetry Festival Organizer, Host Sausalito Sunset Poetry by the Bay, Vice-Chairman Marin Poetry Center, Author of seventeen poetry chapbooks

Be willing, dear readers, to slither through a poetic mudslide of messy truth, where you will find a mighty lotus blooming from the depth of what it takes to rise toward the light in the darkest of times. Blake sheds her grief and anger with beauty and candor, supernatural power, grit, and wit, sounding the alarm for those who have ears to hear this poet's calling, to join the courageous in personal and collective liberation.

> ~ Tonijean Bernbaum, Co-Founder Spirit House Center for Attitudinal Healing, Poet, Ceremonialist

Blake More's spirited poems are resonant musings that dive into the heart of the times when we were all faced with a pandemic that shifted our lives, making many aspects of it unrecognizable. Begging us to question the medical, political and cultural narratives that have unfolded around us, her writing is fierce, passionate and darkly humorous, yet always reverent about the earth we share and woven together with love. Through her poems, we visit the personal, local and global difficulties we're up against in these strange times as sanity looks to be slipping away from all of us. While openly expressing such dislocation, her words are a source of encouragement, hope and truth, reminding us that there is beauty in our world that needs saving.

> ~ Penelope Mclean, International Chef & Art Consultant NOLA

Made in the USA
Middletown, DE
12 July 2024

57162613R00059